AF574856

My Favourite BETJEMAN

The Editors of this book

gratefully acknowledge the generous permission

of the

Literary Executors and the Trustees

of the

Estate of Sir John Betjeman

for the printing here of poems from Sir John's books

"*Collected Poems*" and "*Uncollected Poems*"

published by John Murray (Publishers) Ltd

and for the help and guidance of Mr John Murray C.B.E.

ISBN 0 947987 02 9 Softback

ISBN 0 947987 03 7 Hardback

Lanthorn Limited, 23 Greenwich High Road, London SE10 8JL

Sir Geoffrey Howe

Lady Wilson

Lord Murray

Prunella Scales

Daphne du Maurier

My Favourite BETJEMAN

A selection of his poems by a selection of admirers

Compiled and Edited by
Anthony Kilmister
and Donald Lenox

Foreword by Her Majesty
Queen Elizabeth The Queen Mother
Afterword by
Candida Lycett Green

DRAWINGS AND LETTERING BY KEN WILSON

DESIGNED AND PRODUCED
FOR THE BENEFIT OF THE
PARKINSON'S DISEASE SOCIETY
BY LANTHORN OF LONDON

Kingsley Amis

Sir John Gielgud

Sir Hugh Casson

Thora Hird

Barry Humphries

Mike Yarwood

Virginia Wade

Dr Robert Runcie

Professor Marsden

CLARENCE HOUSE
S.W. 1

It gives me much pleasure to be associated with this book which is being produced to do honour to Sir John Betjeman.

Sir John was a Poet Laureate whose personality, poems and prose touched the lives of countless people in countries far and wide throughout the world. He poked gentle fun at the pompous, while capturing the English way of life of both yesterday and today.

In his last years Parkinson's Disease cast a shadow over his life but

"with sunshine struggling through the mist"

he helped his fellow sufferers by his support of the Parkinson's Disease Society - and yet more than that, he gave them hope and encouragement.

I trust that this volume will give continuing pleasure to all who read it, just as Sir John's life and work gave such pleasure to all who met him or saw him on television or read his very special poetry.

ELIZABETH R
Queen Mother

Dedication

Poems, unlike the books in which they appear, are born not made. The poet gives birth to his creation from his soul, having serviced his muse with talent. In compiling a collection of poems to pay tribute to the poet we had to rely on a little intuition, a lot of luck and on the generosity of those who have given time and thought to choosing a favourite poem and saying why.

These admirers of Sir John, from differing walks of life, speak for the nation, for here was a universally popular poet. With an instinct, an astuteness and a depth which was tempered by the common touch he constantly reminds us of permanent values and through his poems he rubbed elbows with all – from the rich man in his castle to the poor man at his gate.

The idiom employed, the everyday words and the parables of English life which will long be savoured are due to the special stature and flair which Sir John Betjeman possessed and in recognising all this we humbly but affectionately dedicate this book to his memory.

Anthony Kilmister and Don Lenox

Contents

Sir John Betjeman (1906 - 1984)

Reflections by Anthony Kilmister

At the end of a tiring half day's "shooting" for television in his Chelsea home, his secretary Liz Moore and I helped Sir John Betjeman to reach the kitchen where chilled champagne lurked in the refrigerator. Although I was in touch with him on a number of occasions thereafter, this was one of my last face-to-face encounters. The memory of him sipping champagne at the kitchen table will always remain with me.

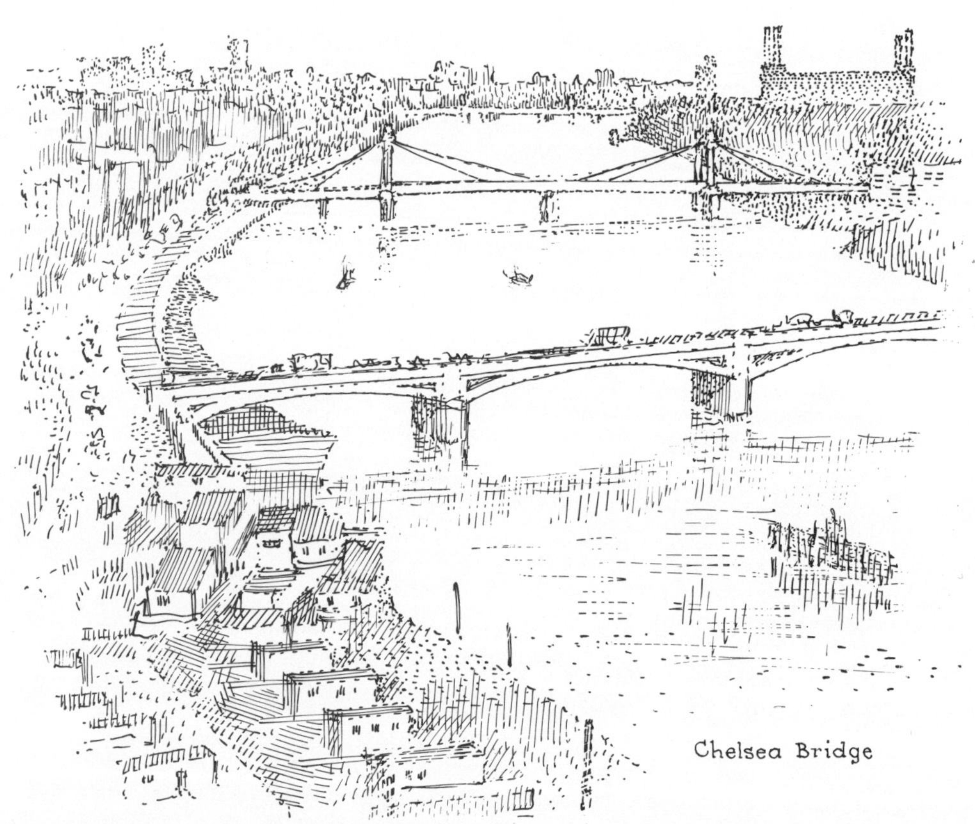

Chelsea Bridge

John Betjeman was born in North West London on 28th. August 1906. Some mystery surrounds the nationality of his ancestors – German or Dutch being the likeliest possibilities.

In the 18th and 19th centuries they settled in a part of London then much favoured by European immigrants and coincidentally where James Parkinson then practiced medicine. Indeed many of Sir John's ancestors were baptised, married and buried at St. Leonard's, Shoreditch, where James Parkinson was church warden.

In "Summoned by Bells" published in 1960 Betjeman describes the first night of term at his Public School - Marlborough - to which he went in 1920.

"Doom! Shivering doom! Clutching a leather grip
Containing things for the first night of term
House slippers, sponge bag, pyjamas, Common Prayer

My health certificate, photographs of home
Where were my bike, my playbox and my trunk?
I walked with strangers down the hill to school
The town's first gaslights twinkled in the cold."

Marlborough

In the autumn of 1925 John Betjeman became an undergraduate at Magdalen College, Oxford, where he was one of a brilliant generation that was to make a name for itself in succeeding years.

Magdalen

The first of Betjeman's numerous books of Poems, "Mount Zion" was published in 1931. In 1933 his prose style was exhibited in "Ghastly Good Taste". At the back of this book was a long fold-out illustration by Peter Fleetwood-Hesketh extended to 9ft. in 1970 when the book was re-published by the illustrator's nephew-by-marriage, Anthony Blond.

Although Betjeman was to become well-known after the Second World War as a television personality as early as 1938 he was "on the telly at Ally Pally".

During the Second World War, after serving as Press Attaché at our embassy in Dublin, Betjeman returned to the Ministry of Information where a girl from Aldershot caught his attention and was immortalised as Joan Hunter Dunn.

In the post War years while book reviewing, broadcasting and writing poetry Betjeman gained an increasing reputation as the patron saint of conservationists. On television this loveable, ramshackle enthusiast whom *The Times* described as Teddy Bear to the nation, alerted us to the joys of old churches, of railway branch lines, of old time Music Hall, of Metro-land. Many people who had never read his poems warmed to his familiar figure on the screen.

Oakworth

Archibald

His "Collected Poems" (1958) sold in its thousands undoubtedly pleasing his publisher John Murray who had been publishing Betjeman's output ever since "Continual Dew" in 1937.

Sir John was knighted in 1969 and made Poet Laureate in 1972. He had an enormous capacity for appreciating English parish churches and I was most grateful to him when he wrote the commendation which appeared on the cover of my own "Good Church Guide".

By this time he was suffering from Parkinson's Disease but his kindly, somewhat eccentric personality, his instinctive appreciation of all that is best in England's heritage and his sense of fun continued to brighten the lives of his contemporaries.

They were like the bubbles in the champagne.

St John's, Oxford

Kingsley Amis

This is not one of the best known of John's poems but it has always been a favourite of mine because it illustrates so well his marvellous power of moving from ordinary life to something sublime in just a few words. One moment a commonplace little man is knocking his golf-ball along and the next there is 'splendour everywhere' - real splendour too, beautifully imagined and put together. (I am no golfer myself, by the way.) Like that little man, the reader is not quite sure how he has arrived at this blissful state.

Seaside Golf

How straight it flew, how long it flew,
  It clear'd the rutty track
And soaring, disappeared from view
  Beyond the bunker's back –
A glorious, sailing, bounding drive
That made me glad I was alive.

And down the fairway, far along
  It glowed a lonely white;
I played an iron sure and strong
  And clipp'd it out of sight,
And spite of grassy banks between
I knew I'd find it on the green.

And so I did. It lay content
  Two paces from the pin;
A steady putt and then it went
  Oh, most securely in.
The very turf rejoiced to see
That quite unprecedented three.

Ah! seaweed smells from sandy caves
  And thyme and mist in whiffs,
In-coming tide, Atlantic waves
  Slapping the sunny cliffs,
Lark song and sea sounds in the air
And splendour, splendour everywhere.

St. Enodoc

Harrow-on-the-Hill

Sir Hugh Casson

Everybody finds what they look for in the poetry of John Betjeman – compassion, humility, joy in ordinary people and simple facts, humour, gentleness, fear of mortality, love of landscape and buildings, poetic craftsmanship, anger tragedy or loneliness. What I look for, find and admire is his needle-sharp observation and his sense of place – the inglenook of a teashop, the ward of a cottage hospital, a suburban road, a bed-sitter or a village church. Nothing escapes that bright and tender eye – so although of all his poems I have probably enjoyed most his blank verse autobiography "Summoned by Bells", for this anthology I would choose (with difficulty) between "Youth and Age on the Beaulieu River", (where I have spent much of my own youth and age), "Business Girls", "Trebetherick", "Parliament Hill Fields"... and first of all perhaps "Harrow-on-the-Hill"... a masterpiece.

Harrow-on-the-Hill

When melancholy Autumn comes to Wembley
  And electric trains are lighted after tea
The poplars near the Stadium are trembly
  With their tap and tap and whispering to me,
    Like the sound of little breakers
    Spreading out along the surf-line
When the estuary's filling
        With the sea.

Then Harrow-on-the-Hill's a rocky island
  And Harrow churchyard full of sailors' graves
And the constant click and kissing of the trolley buses hissing
  Is the level to the Wealdstone turned to waves
    And the rumble of the railway
    Is the thunder of the rollers
As they gather up for plunging
        Into caves.

There's a storm cloud to the westward over Kenton,
  There's a line of harbour lights at Perivale,
Is it rounding rough Pentire in a flood of sunset fire
  The little fleet of trawlers under sail?
    Can those boats be only roof tops
    As they stream along the skyline
In a race for port and Padstow
        With the gale?

Padstow Harbour

Daphne du Maurier

"Cornish Cliffs" appeals to me very much because of my love for Cornwall which has been my home for nearly all of my life.

Cornwall

Cornish Cliffs

Those moments, tasted once and never done,
Of long surf breaking in the mid-day sun.
A far-off blow-hole booming like a gun—

The seagulls plane and circle out of sight
Below this thirsty, thrift-encrusted height,
The veined sea-campion buds burst into white

And gorse turns tawny orange, seen beside
Pale drifts of primroses cascading wide
To where the slate falls sheer into the tide.

More than in gardened Surrey, nature spills
A wealth of heather, kidney-vetch and squills
Over these long-defended Cornish hills.

A gun-emplacement of the latest war
Looks older than the hill fort built before
Saxon or Norman headed for the shore.

And in the shadowless, unclouded glare
Deep blue above us fades to whiteness where
A misty sea-line meets the wash of air.

Nut-smell of gorse and honey-smell of ling
Waft out to sea the freshness of the spring
On sunny shallows, green and whispering.

The wideness which the lark-song gives the sky
Shrinks at the clang of sea-birds sailing by
Whose notes are tuned to days when seas are high.

From today's calm, the lane's enclosing green
Leads inland to a usual Cornish scene—
Slate cottages with sycamore between,

Small fields and tellymasts and wires and poles
With, as the everlasting ocean rolls,
Two chapels built for half a hundred souls

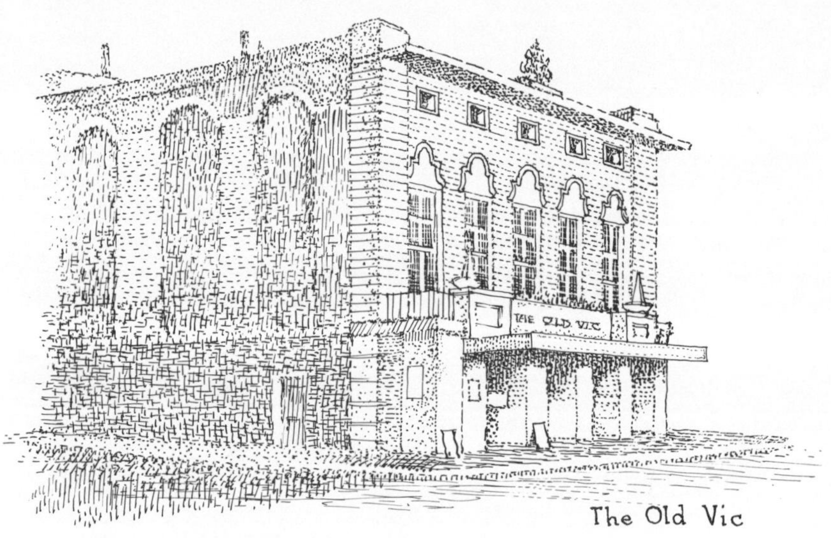

The Old Vic

Sir John Gielgud

As one grows in to old age, one is increasingly haunted by the plight of contemporaries who suffer from the onslaught of disease and helplessness, especially, of course, when the sufferers are friends or relatives whom one has known in good health for many years. In my own profession, my brother Val, Sir Michael Redgrave, Kenneth More and Lord Olivier (though he continues to battle on with unfailing courage and determination) have all been stricken in recent years and been gradually forced to cease leading active and purposeful lives.

In other fields, Sir Cecil Beaton, Sir Osbert Sitwell and Sir John Betjeman all fought to retain their faculties as long as possible. But the touching poem I have chosen called "Loneliness" gives some hint of Betjeman's struggles and personal wretchedness in his long illness. It is bad enough to lose one's friends by death, but the unexpected blows that cripple the lives of one's friends in their old age are a continued reminder to us all of the cruel years of disablement that lie in wait so wretchedly for those whom fate strikes down.

Beech Woods

Loneliness

The last year's leaves are on the beech:
    The twigs are black; the cold is dry;
To deeps beyond the deepest reach
    The Easter bells enlarge the sky.
O ordered metal clatter-clang!
Is yours the song the angels sang?
You fill my heart with joy and grief –
Belief! Belief! And unbelief...
    And, though you tell me I shall die,
    You say not how or when or why.

Indifferent the finches sing,
    Unheeding roll the lorries past:
What misery will this year bring
    Now spring is in the air at last?
For, sure as blackthorn bursts to snow,
Cancer in some of us will grow,
The tasteful crematorium door
Shuts out for some the furnace roar;
    But church bells open on the blast
    Our loneliness, so long and vast.

Morecambe

Thora Hird

I enjoy so many of John Betjeman's poems that I find it difficult to choose a favourite one. Being a person who wallows in nostalgia it is obvious that "Thoughts on 'The Diary of a Nobody'" is a favourite of mine ... yet "The Retired Postal Clerk" is *so* moving – I feel it must be my favourite choice.

With many other poets one thinks – "Oh what wonderfully unique thoughts", whereas with Betjeman one could always identify with his thoughts and feel he had written just what *you* would have thought and said!

So – thank you dear John Betjeman
  for hours of gentle pleasure.
Your magic pen has brought to us –
  affection beyond measure.
Your warm defensive attitude –
  when *change* did not mean *better*
Your quiet voice – that proved its point –
  sincerely – to the letter.
So – no goodbyes – John Betjeman
  for nothing can we sever,
You haven't *really* left us –
  for your words will live forever!

The Retired Postal Clerk

Since the wife died the house seems lonely-like,
It isn't quite the same place as before;
Ron's got the garage for his motor-bike —
I didn't want the Morris any more.

Ron's wife's the trouble. When I said to her,
'Why don't you come and settle here with Ron?'
She flat refused. You'd think she would prefer
A bigger place, with mother being gone.

But not a bit of it : and all she said
Was, 'What I want's a place to call my own' —
She meant that she could wait till I was dead;
So here I am, just living all alone.

I sold the Morris out Benhilton way —
I couldn't keep it in this summer weather —
That empty seat beside me all the day;
Along the roads we used to go together

Out to Carshalton Beeches for a spin
And back by Chislehurst and Bromley town,
Where Mum would have her lemon juice and gin
And I would have a half of old and brown —
And those last months when she was really bad,
They were the only pleasures that she had.

Bromley

Sir Geoffrey Howe

"The Wykehamist" is vintage Betjeman.

Vintage in its accuracy of perception: one of my Ministerial colleagues at the Treasury provoked never ending astonishment by his "appearance on his bike".

Vintage in its provocative criticism - and yet not *quite* unjust: "rather dirty" goes too far, I like to think, for most of us; but our hush puppy informality *does* fall happily short of Etonian elegance.

Vintage in its affectionate praise: yes, we do "go full pelt" for our often eccentric wants.

Vintage too in its capacity to stir long forgotten memories : "St Mary calls above the mellow college walls" with such renewed clarity that chapel clock is ringing again in my ears, after four decades of silence.

And inevitably a touch of mystery : why on earth, one wonders, the dedication to Randolph Churchill?

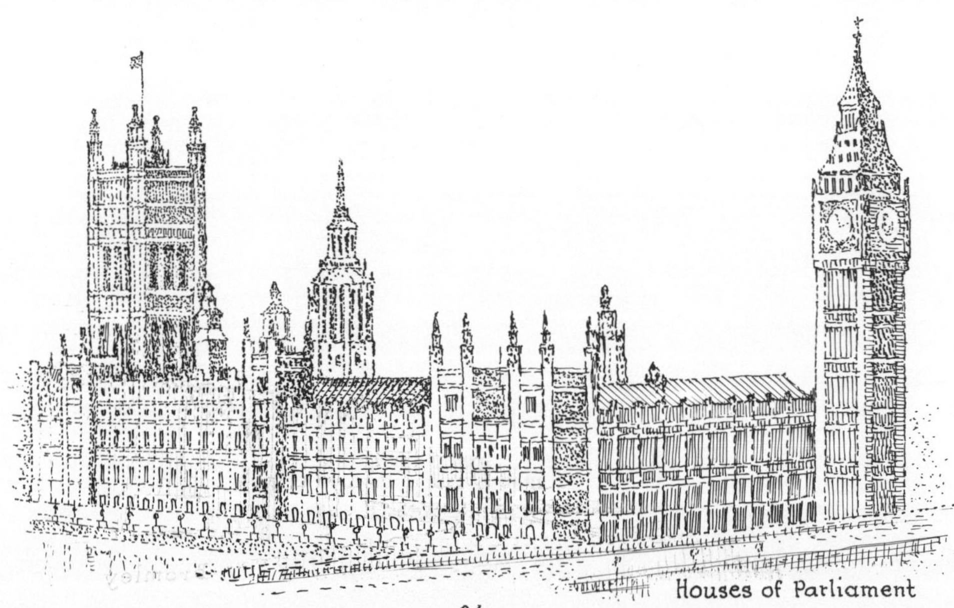

Houses of Parliament

Winchester College

The Wykehamist

(To Randolph Churchill,
but not about him.)

Broad of Church and broad of mind,
Broad before and broad behind,
A keen ecclesiologist,
A rather dirty Wykehamist.
'Tis not for us to wonder why
He wears that curious knitted tie;
We should not cast reflections on
The very slightest kind of don.
We should not giggle as we like
At his appearance on his bike;
It's something to become a bore,
And more than that, at twenty-four.
It's something too to know your wants
And go full pelt for Norman fonts.
Just now the chestnut trees are dark
And full with shadow in the park,
And "six o'clock!" St. Mary calls
Above the mellow college walls.
The evening stretches arms to twist
And captivate her Wykehamist
But not for him these autumn days,
He shuts them out with heavy baize;
He gives his Ovaltine a stir
And nibbles at a "petit beurre",
And, satisfying fleshy wants,
He settles down to Norman fonts.

Barry Humphries

This is the only poem which John wrote about my homeland and it is mostly about jet travel, helpful hostesses, in-flight snacks and a yearning for Cornwall. His wonderful films about Australia aside, it is a pity that he was not inspired to verse by his two visits down under, although in the early sixties he did write a very funny conjectural prose-poem about Kangaroo Island in South Australia, a place he never visited. It appeared in a travel magazine and I hope some diligent anthologist discovers it.

Soon after meeting John I went for a holiday in Cornwall on his recommendation and accidentally fell off a cliff near Zennor. I was rescued by what appeared to be the entire cast of the Pirates of Penzance and I starred on the front pages of several London 'dailies' being winched off a ledge by a chopper.

While in hospital in London, John visited me and was relieved to learn that my physio bore the apposite Cornish patronym Tregenza.

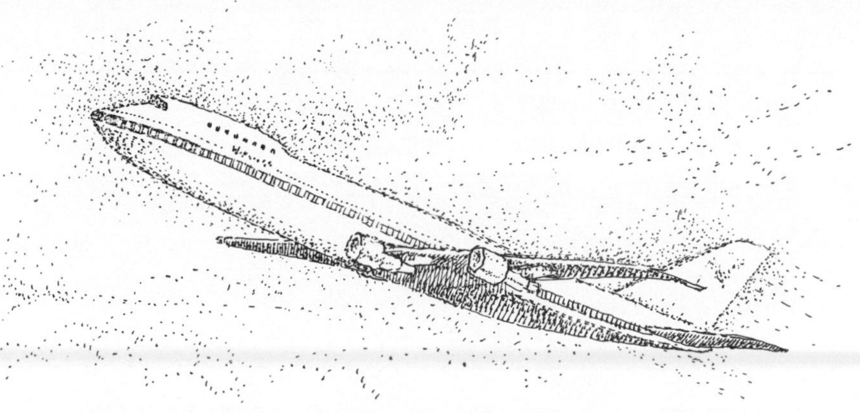

Back from Australia

Cocooned in Time, at this inhuman height,
The packaged food tastes neutrally of clay.
We never seem to catch the running day
But travel on in everlasting night
With all the chic accoutrements of flight:
Lotions and essences in neat array
And yet another plastic cup and tray.
'Thank you *so* much. Oh no, I'm quite all right.'

At home in Cornwall hurrying autumn skies
Leave Bray Hill barren, Stepper jutting bare,
And hold the moon above the sea-wet sand.
The very last of late September dies
In frosty silence and the hills declare
How vast the sky is, looked at from the land.

Polzeath

Professor David Marsden

There is something delightfully athletic and evocative about "A Subaltern's Love Song" in which Sir John Betjeman conjures up not only a day dream about Miss Joan Hunter Dunn but also the strenuous singles played after tea.

It is sad to think that many Parkinson's Disease patients – one of whom Sir John was later to become – are unable to participate in such sporting activity. Parkinson's Disease can be a most disabling illness and this is precisely why the Society, in aid of which this collection of poems is being sold, is combating the condition with such enthusiasm and vigour.

To Sir John the Society owes much – for it was his appearance on BBC television in December 1981 which launched a national appeal eventually making possible the creation of a Parkinson's Disease Society Research Centre in South East London. It is here that my laboratories are located.

He lived to know that those laboratories were opened by Princess Margaret in May 1984 and I like to think he was as enthusiastic about that as he was about tennis with Miss Joan Hunter Dunn.

Parkinson's Disease Society
Research Centre

A Subaltern's Love Song

Miss J. Hunter Dunn, Miss J. Hunter Dunn,
Furnish'd and burnish'd by Aldershot sun,
What strenuous singles we played after tea,
We in the tournament—you against me!

Love-thirty, love-forty, oh! weakness of joy,
The speed of a swallow, the grace of a boy,
With carefullest carelessness, gaily you won,
I am weak from your loveliness, Joan Hunter Dunn.

Miss Joan Hunter Dunn, Miss Joan Hunter Dunn,
How mad I am, sad I am, glad that you won.
The warm-handled racket is back in its press,
But my shock-headed victor, she loves me no less.

Her father's euonymus shines as we walk,
And swing past the summer-house, buried in talk,
And cool the verandah that welcomes us in
To the six-o'clock news and a lime-juice and gin.

The scent of the conifers, sound of the bath,
The view from my bedroom of moss-dappled path,
As I struggle with double-end evening tie,
For we dance at the Golf Club, my victor and I.

On the floor of her bedroom lie blazer and shorts
And the cream-coloured walls are be-trophied with sports,
And westering, questioning settles the sun
On your low-leaded window, Miss Joan Hunter Dunn.

The Hillman is waiting, the light's in the hall,
The pictures of Egypt are bright on the wall,
My sweet, I am standing beside the oak stair
And there on the landing's the light on your hair.

By roads "not adopted", by woodlanded ways,
She drove to the club in the late summer haze,
Into nine-o'clock Camberley, heavy with bells
And mushroomy, pine-woody, evergreen smells.

Miss Joan Hunter Dunn, Miss Joan Hunter Dunn,
I can hear from the car-park the dance has begun.
Oh! full Surrey twilight! importunate band!
Oh! strongly adorable tennis-girl's hand!

Around us are Rovers and Austins afar,
Above us, the intimate roof of the car,
And here on my right is the girl of my choice,
With the tilt of her nose and the chime of her voice,

And the scent of her wrap, and the words never said,
And the ominous, ominous dancing ahead.
We sat in the car park till twenty to one
And now I'm engaged to Miss Joan Hunter Dunn.

Hillman

Lord Murray

There is a becoming modesty about Shropshire itself which prompts in its lads (and wenches - not lasses) mixed feelings about what others write of us. We are grateful for being noticed at all, but apprehensive lest being noticed should be the first step to being spoiled.

That this poem should remind the world of one of Shropshire's heroes must then be - to me at least - a reason for commending it. Pleasing too to see in print (in a poetry-book at that!) the place-names of one's boyhood - Oakengates and Coalbrookdale, echoes of Clunton and Clunbury. Linking familiar arms in his practised way with his reader, Betjeman evokes memories and associations which amplify and enhance his own lines.

And again, as so often with Betjeman, his friendly and reassuring arm on yours, he guides you from the prosaic gaslamps and housebacks to the surreal Webb in a water sheeting - but gently, acceptably, even comfortably.

But - only "Captain Webb - the swimmer"? Not "the first man to swim the Channel"? Modest we may be in Shropshire, but not as modest as all that.

Coalbrookdale

A Shropshire Lad

The gas was on in the Institute,
The flare was up in the gym,
A man was running a mineral line,
A lass was singing a hymn,
When Captain Webb the Dawley man,
Captain Webb from Dawley,
Came swimming along the old canal
That carried the bricks to Lawley.
Swimming along —
Swimming along —
Swimming along from Severn,
And paying a call at Dawley Bank while swimming along to Heaven.

The sun shone low on the railway line
And over the bricks and stacks,
And in at the upstairs windows
of the Dawley houses' backs,
When we saw the ghost of Captain Webb,
Webb in a water sheeting,
Come dripping along in a bathing dress
To the Saturday evening meeting.
Dripping along —
Dripping along —
To the Congregational Hall ;
Dripping and still he rose over the sill and faded away in a wall.

There wasn't a man in Oakengates
That hadn't got hold of the tale,
And over the valley in Ironbridge,
And round by Coalbrookdale,
How Captain Webb the Dawley man,
Captain Webb from Dawley
Rose rigid and dead from the old canal
That carries the bricks to Lawley,
Rigid and dead —
Rigid and dead —
To the Saturday congregation,
Paying a call at Dawley Bank on his way to his destination.

Prunella Scales

This is not, I suppose, John Betjeman's most profound or "important" poem, but I like it for the extreme niceness of the lady who has never heard of him and the extreme awfulness of all the other people who have; for the ingenious internal rhymes which are so unforced you can miss many of them on first reading; because it is touching as well as funny; and for the fact that if you read it aloud (like so many of the poems for which we actors bless John Betjeman's memory), it is hugely enjoyed by even the stickiest audience.

Abinger

Reproof Deserved
or
After the Lecture

When I saw the grapefruit drying, cherry in each centre
lying,
And a dozen guests expected at the table's polished oak,
Then I knew, my lecture finished, I'ld be feeling quite
diminished
Talking on, but unprotected, so that all my spirit broke.

"Have you read the last Charles Morgan?" "Are you
writing for the organ
Which is published as a vital adjunct to our cultural
groups?"
"This year some of us are learning all *The Lady's Not for
Burning*
For a poetry recital we are giving to the troops."

"Mr Betjeman, I grovel before critics of the novel,
Tell me, if I don't offend you, have you written one your-
self?
You haven't? Then the one I wrote is (not that I expect a
notice)
Something I would like to send you, just for keeping on
your shelf."
"Betjeman, I bet your racket brings you in a pretty packet
Raising the old lecture curtain, writing titbits here and
there.
But, by Jove, your hair is thinner, since you came to us in
Pinner,
And you're fatter now, I'm certain. What you need is
country air."

This and that way conversation, till I turn in desperation
To a kind face (can I doubt it?) mercifully mute so far.
"Oh," it says, "I missed the lecture, wasn't it on archi-
tecture?
Do please tell me all about it, what you do and who you
are."

Virginia Wade

Having always been an admirer of Sir John Betjeman's poetry, it is personally thrilling to know that he was such an ardent tennis enthusiast. I particularly like "The Olympic Girl", where he ascribes a sensuality not only to the exalted player, but also to the instrument of the trade, the racket. The intimate relationship between a player and a racket, which ideally becomes an extension of the body, is totally understood and personalised by him.

Wimbledon

The Olympic Girl

The sort of girl I like to see
Smiles down from her great height at me.
She stands in strong, athletic pose
And wrinkles her *retroussé* nose.
Is it distaste that makes her frown,
So furious and freckled, down
On an unhealthy worm like me ?
Or am I what she likes to see?
I do not know, though much I care.
ειθε γενηίοην... would I were
(Forgive me, shade of Rupert Brooke)
An object fit to claim her look.
Oh! would I were her racket press'd
With hard excitement to her breast
And swished into the sunlit air
Arm-high above her tousled hair,
And banged against the bounding ball
"Oh! Plung!" my taughten'd strings would call
"Oh! Plung! my darling, break my strings

For you I will do brilliant things."
And when the match is over, I
Would flop beside you, hear you sigh;
And then, with what supreme caress,
You'ld tuck me up into my press.
Fair tigress of the tennis courts,
So short in sleeve and strong in shorts,
Little, alas, to you I mean,
For I am bald and old and green.

Lady Wilson

I have chosen this poem because it captures vividly the images and attitudes of the thirties and early forties - Bravington rings, Warwick Deeping (probably the beautifully dated "Sorrell and Son").

The girl is brought to life as one of the gallery of "Betjeman girls". I can see her hair as a mass of sculptured curls, and she is wearing a tailored tweed suit, and seamed silk stockings, and brogue shoes with a tongue flap.

She calmly keeps her suitors at bay, for she hopes for the love of the Air Vice-Marshal of the 'drome.

Station Siren

She sat with a Warwick Deeping,
  Her legs curl'd round in a ring,
Like a beautiful panther sleeping,
  Yet always ready to spring.

Tweed on her well-knit torso,
  Silk on each big strong leg,
An officer's lady - and more so
  Than those who buy off the peg.

More cash than she knew of for spending
  As a Southgate girl at home,
For there's crooning and clinging unending
  For the queen of the girls at the 'drome.

Beautiful brown eyes burning
  Deep on the Deeping page,
Beautiful dark hair learning
  Coiffuring tricks of the age.

Negligent hand for holding
  A Flight-Lieutenant at bay,
Petulant lips for scolding
  And kissing the trouble away.

But she isn't exactly partial
  To any of that sort of thing,
So maybe the Air Vice-Marshal
  Will buy her a Bravington ring.

Mike Yarwood

It's very difficult to choose just one of Sir John Betjeman's poems as a favourite, there are so many that I enjoy. However, I can't help smiling as I read "How to Get On in Society", I think there's a little bit of us all there. Eager to please, but aware of our own shortcomings.

The London Palladium

How to Get On in Society

Originally set as a competition in "Time and Tide"

Phone for the fish knives, Norman
  As Cook is a little unnerved;
You kiddies have crumpled the serviettes
  And I must have things daintily served.

Are the requisites all in the toilet?
  The frills round the cutlets can wait
Till the girl has replenished the cruets
  And switched on the logs in the grate.

It's ever so close in the lounge, dear,
  But the vestibule's comfy for tea
And Howard is out riding on horseback
  So do come and take some with me.

Now here is a fork for your pastries
  And do use the couch for your feet;
I know what I wanted to ask you—
  Is trifle sufficient for sweet?

Milk and then just as it comes dear?
  I'm afraid the preserve's full of stones;
Beg pardon, I'm soiling the doileys
  With afternoon tea-cakes and scones.

The Archbishop of Canterbury

When John Betjeman walked into the Archbishop's Chapel on one of his visits to Lambeth, I vividly remember him exclaiming - "Wonderful. I suppose that this is our Sistine Chapel". It was a startling pronouncement. Most people are apt to dismiss the Chapel as commonplace. The poet was not however being satirical and so powerful was his sense of place and historical association that those who stood with him saw the Chapel in a new and richer light.

Later on the same day he was found in the Victorian part of the Palace chanting the praises of the architect — "Good old Blore"! Affection, wonder and an apparent simplicity which cloaked deep wisdom and a mature, well tested Christian faith - I remember John Betjeman for all these qualities and more. He is powerfully present for me when I read his poem, "Christmas".

Lambeth Palace

Christmas

The bells of waiting Advent ring,
  The tortoise stove is lit again
And lamp-oil light across the night
  Has caught the streaks of winter rain
In many a stained glass window sheen
From Crimson Lake to Hooker's Green.

The holly in the windy hedge
  And round the Manor House the yew
Will soon be stripped to deck the ledge,
  The altar, font and arch and pew,
So that the villagers can say
'The church looks nice' on Christmas Day.

Provincial public houses blaze
  And Corporation tramcars clang,
On lighted tenements I gaze
  Where paper decorations hang,
And bunting in the red Town Hall
Says 'Merry Christmas to you all.'

And London shops on Christmas Eve
  Are strung with silver bells and flowers
As hurrying clerks the City leave
  To pigeon-haunted classic towers,
And marbled clouds go scudding by
The many-steepled London sky.

And girls in slacks remember Dad,
And oafish louts remember Mum,
And sleepless children's hearts are glad,
  And Christmas-morning bells say 'Come!'
Even to shining ones who dwell
Safe in the Dorchester Hotel.

And is it true? And is it true,
  This most tremendous tale of all,
Seen in a stained-glass window's hue,
  A Baby in an ox's stall?
The maker of the stars and sea
Become a Child on earth for me?

And is it true? For if it is,
  No loving fingers tying strings
Around those tissued fripperies,
  The sweet and silly Christmas things,
Bath salts and inexpensive scent
And hideous tie so kindly meant,

No love that in a family dwells,
  No carolling in frosty air,
Nor all the steeple-shaking bells
  Can with this simple truth compare -
That God was Man in Palestine
And lives today in Bread and Wine.

Canterbury

Afterword by Candida Lycett Green

Although my father was aware in his lifetime of the broad range of his readership as shown by the sale of his books and by the letters he received, he remained constantly amazed at his success. I would like to quote from a letter I received after his death which explains so well why his poetry was so popular:

> "...he had the poet's true gift, that of extending everyone's vision of the poetic and showing us the sanctity of the ordinary. He also wore his mortal frailties, showed us how our failings mustn't be buttoned up or swept under the carpet, and can be put to work. Hymner of doubts and snobberies, lover of roads unadopted, sulky blondes, north Oxford, the Church of England, lesbian chicken farmers, more than anyone I can think of did he bring the beam of love and understanding into dim corners...."

He would be touched, and his heart warmed to see the diversity of poems selected by these contributors, all distinguished in their separate callings whether from church, government, industry, the theatrical world, sport or literature. To read why they like a particular poem reveals something of them and the extent to which my father's words evoked a response in so diverse a circle.

He would be pleased, too, to know that the sales of this slim volume are to benefit both the Research and Welfare activities of the Parkinson's Disease Society. All those who have taken part in this unique tribute to my father by choosing a poem or purchasing the book have by so doing helped all those sufferers in the United Kingdom afflicted by Parkinson's Disease.

My father spoke with feeling about his Parkinsonism on television when seeking support for the Society. He recalled that the Shaking Palsy as James Parkinson (1755-1824) described it in 1817 was known in Biblical times but he said that shaking is

> "Only the most visible symptom of Parkinson's Disease; it is not the worst. I know, I've got it myself. Being unable to move your limbs at all or at best with difficulty; being unable to cross a room let alone a street without "freezing"; being always terrified lest you fall. These are far worse, and made more terrible by the fact that whilst our bodies fail us our minds remain alert and we are aware of our deterioration. I am not suffering from some rare disease; there are more than 100,000 others like me in this country alone. The older you get, the more likely you are to develop the disease. I was 68 when it was diagnosed. The main hope for all of us lies with the Parkinson's Disease Society. They give advice and help, both to sufferers and their families. They also sponsor research at such places as the laboratories in South East London run by Professor Marsden".

Those words provoked an enormous response and are still remembered by fellow Parkinsonians today. But the memories I treasure are of the happy carefree years in which he was not only the best father in the world, but also my best friend. He taught me to look at everything twice, and if I have inherited *anything* from him it is the pleasure of observation not only in buildings, but in people too. "Church crawling" was part of our lives, and journeys from Berkshire to Cornwall in the holidays often took three or four days as a result. The tiny church at Trebetherick was always and now remains the last and happiest port of call.

"Blessed be St. Enodoc, blessed be the wave,
Blessed be the springy turf, we pray, we pray to thee,
Ask for our children all the happy days you gave...."

St. Enodoc,
Trebetherick

John Betjeman Titles In Print

BETJEMAN'S CORNWALL · Betjeman

CHURCH POEMS · Betjeman

COLLECTED POEMS · Betjeman

SUMMONED BY BELLS · Betjeman

UNCOLLECTED POEMS · Betjeman

BETJEMAN COUNTRY · Delaney

JOHN BETJEMAN : A LIFE IN PICTURES - Bevis Hillier

HIGH & LOW - Betjeman

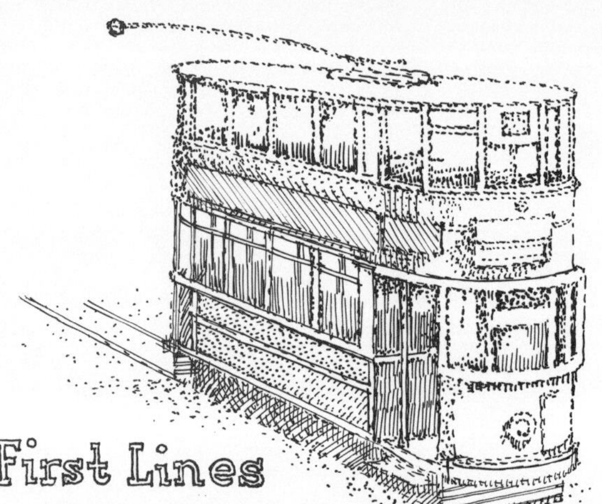

Index of First Lines

Acknowledgements

This book would not have been possible without the generous support of the Literary Executors and the Trustees of the Estate of the late Sir John Betjeman. Their permission to print poems by Sir John and the warm co-operation of Mr John Murray CBE will be of enormous benefit to the Parkinson's Disease Society in aid of which this book is being sold. The poems selected are from either *Collected Poems* or *Uncollected Poems* both of which are published by John Murray (Publishers) Ltd whose co-operation also is very greatly valued.

Photograph credits :

H.M. Queen Elizabeth The Queen Mother - Camera Press
Kingsley Amis – Hutchinson Publishing Group
Sir Hugh Casson - Paul Caffell
Thora Hird - BBC
Sir Geoffrey Howe — London Pictures Service
Barry Humphries – William Morris Agency
Professor Marsden – Pic Photos
Lord Murray – Brian Worth
Sir John Betjeman – John Murray
Candida Lycett Green – Hamish Hamilton

For help received in a variety of ways we are grateful to a host of people and organizations, not least Mr Blair Eames of Social Service Advertising Limited and Nationwide Building Society.

Ken Wilson's thanks to Sheila Dunn for assistance with the preparation work.

The Euston Arch

ORDER FORM

A new book in tribute to the late Poet Laureate, Sir John Betjeman,
in aid of the
Parkinson's Disease Society of the United Kingdom

"MY FAVOURITE BETJEMAN:"
A selection of his poems by a selection of admirers

Foreword by
Her Majesty Queen Elizabeth The Queen Mother

Fourteen distinguished contributors from a variety of callings have chosen their favourite poem by John Betjeman and have told why they have chosen it. This enchanting book with more than 30 illustrations will give continuing pleasure to all who read it, just as Sir John's life and work gave such pleasure to all who met him, saw him on television or read his very special poetry. Modestly priced, it will make an excellent gift. The entire proceeds are in aid of the Parkinson's Disease Society.

52 pages
Paperback £3.95
Hardback £6.95

Designed and produced for the benefit of the Parkinson's Disease Society by Lanthorn of London

To: Nationwide Building Society, New Oxford House, High Holborn, London WC1V 6PW.

"MY FAVOURITE BETJEMAN: A selection of his poems by a selection of admirers"

Please send me_____copies of the paperback edition @ £3.95 each
Please send me_____copies of the hardback edition @ £6.95 each
I enclose my cheque/Postal Order for £__________
made payable to **Lanthorn of London**

Name____________________

Address____________________

PLEASE PRINT YOUR NAME AND ADDRESS IN FULL AND IN BLOCK CAPITAL LETTERS

New Oxford House, High Holborn, London WC1V 6PW Telephone 01-242 8822

Nationwide Building Society

Member of the Building Societies Association

Chief General Manager
Tim Melville-Ross

April 1985

Mrs V Milne
Messrs Upsdales
8 Wangey Road
Chadwell Heath
Romford
Essex

Dear Mrs Milne

Thank you for your order for "My Favourite Betjeman".

the search for a cure.

If any of your friends would like to obtain a copy, an order form is enclosed to make this easy, and additional forms are available from any branch of Nationwide.

Nationwide Building Society is pleased to be able to assist the Parkinson's Disease Society, and would like to thank you on their behalf for your support.

Yours sincerely

Karin Williams.

Marketing Department